This Book
Belongs To:

....

....

I spy with my little eye something beginning with...

It's an Apple

I spy with my little eye something beginning with...

B

It's a
Bat

I spy with my little eye something beginning with...

It's a Candy

I spy with my little eye something beginning with...

D

It's
Dracula

I spy with my little eye something beginning with...

It's an Eyeball

I spy with my little eye something beginning with...

It's a
Finger

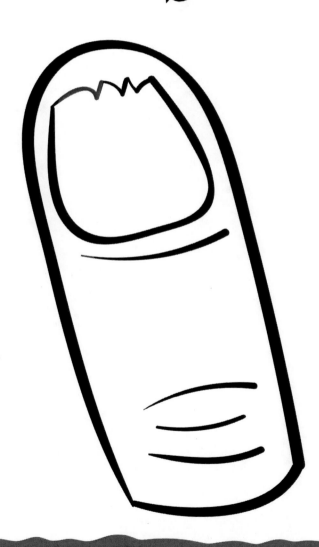

I spy with my little eye something beginning with...

It's a
Ghost

I spy with my little eye something beginning with...

It's a
Hat

I spy with my little eye something beginning with...

I

It's an Ice Cream

I spy with my little eye something beginning with...

It's a
Jar

I spy with my little eye something beginning with...

K

It's a
Kitten

I spy with my little eye something beginning with...

It's a Lantern

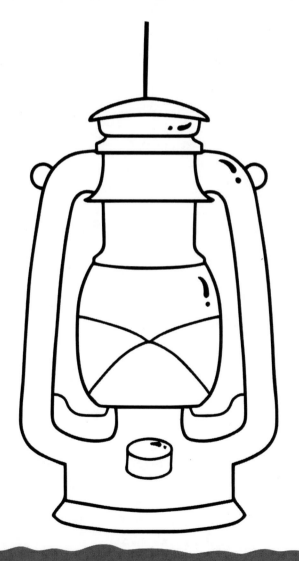

I spy with my little eye something beginning with...

It's a Mummy

I spy with my little eye something beginning with...

It's a Ninja

I spy with my little eye something beginning with...

It's an Owl

I spy with my little eye something beginning with...

It's a
Pumpkin

I spy with my little eye something beginning with...

It's a Queen

I spy with my little eye something beginning with...

It's a
Rat

I spy with my little eye something beginning with...

It's a
Skeleton

I spy with my little eye something beginning with...

It's a
Tombstone

I spy with my little eye something beginning with...

U

It's a Unicorn

I spy with my little eye something beginning with...

It's a
Vampire

I spy with my little eye something beginning with...

It's a Witch

I spy with my little eye something beginning with...

It's a
Xylophone

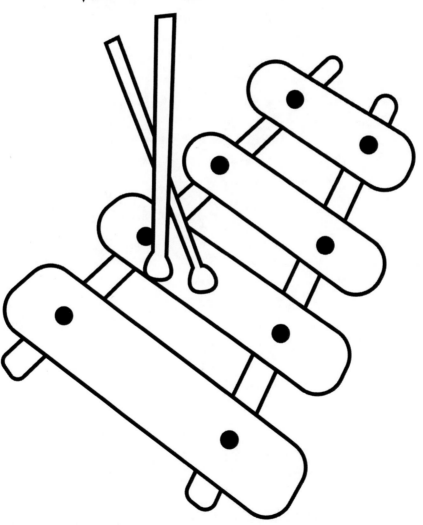

I spy with my little eye something beginning with...

It's a
Yo-yo

I spy with my little eye something beginning with...

It's a
Zombie

Made in United States
North Haven, CT
11 October 2022